Ladybug

**Karen Hartley
and
Chris Macro**

Heinemann Library
Des Plaines, Illinois

© 1998 Reed Educational & Professional Publishing
Published by Heinemann Library,
an imprint of Reed Educational & Professional Publishing,
1350 East Touhy Avenue, Suite 240 West
Des Plaines, IL 60018

Customer Service 1-888-454-2279

Designed by Celia Floyd
Illustrations by Alan Male
Printed in Hong Kong

02 01 00 99
10 9 8 7 6 5 4 3 2

Library of Congress Cataloging-in-Publication Data

Hartley, Karen, 1949-
      Ladybug / Karen Hartley and Chris Macro.
           p.   cm. -- (Bug books)
      Includes bibliographical references and index.
      Summary: A simple introduction to the physical characteristics,
diet, life cycle, predator, habitat, and lifespan of the ladybird
beetle, also known as the ladybug.
       ISBN 1-57572-662-9 (lib. bdg.)
       1. Ladybugs--Juvenile literature. [1. Ladybugs.] I. Macro,
Chris, 1940-. II. Title. III. Series.
      QL596.C65H35   1998
      595.76'9--DC21   98-11616
                                                               CIP
                                                               AC

Paperback ISBN 1-57572-458-8

Acknowledgments
The Publishers would like to thank the following for permission to reproduce photographs: Bubbles: Thurston p. 29; Bruce Coleman: D. Austen p. 25, W. Cheng Ward p. 5, J. Grayson p. 13, P. Kaya pp. 6, 27, H. Reinhard pp. 4, 19, F. Sauer p. 21, K. Taylor pp. 12, 28; NHPA: S. Dalton p. 8, D. Middleton p. 18; Oxford Scientific Films: P. Franklin p. 16, S. Littlewood p. 15, A . MacEwen p. 20, A. Ramage pp. 10, 11, 26, T. Shepherd p. 22; Premaphotos: K. Preston-Mafham pp. 9, 17, 23, 24; Science Photo Library: J Burgess p. 7

Cover photograph reproduced with permission of child; Chris Honeywell, ladybug; C. Nuridsany & M. Peronnou/Science Photo Library

Any words appearing in the text in bold, **like this**, are explained in the Glossary.

Contents

What are ladybugs?

Ladybugs are **insects**. There are over 400 different kinds of ladybugs in North America. There are hundreds more around the world.

Ladybugs are small **beetles** with a round body like half a ball. They have six legs and two pairs of wings. Most are red or yellow with black spots.

What do ladybugs look like?

Some ladybugs are black with red spots and some are black or brown with white spots. We are going to look at red ladybugs with black spots.

Ladybugs have two eyes that can see up, down, backward, and forward at the same time. They have two **antennae** for feeling and two jaws for biting.

How big are ladybugs?

Some kinds of ladybugs are bigger than others. An eyed ladybug, like the one in this picture, is about as long as your little fingernail.

These 16-spot ladybugs are very, very tiny. They are about the same size as the head of a pin!

How are ladybugs born?

In spring and summer the weather is warm and female ladybugs lay eggs on the undersides of leaves. The eggs are **oval** and pale yellow.

After four days a **larva hatches** out of each egg. The larvae are called grubs. Some ladybug larvae have black, pointed bodies and six legs.

How do ladybugs grow?

When the **larvae hatch**, they grow
very quickly and **molt** three times in
three weeks. The larvae turn dark blue
with yellow or red spots.

After four weeks each larva sticks its body to a leaf and turns into a **pupa**. A week later it splits open and out crawls a ladybug. It stretches its wings to dry.

What do ladybugs eat?

Most ladybugs look for tiny green insects called aphids to eat but some kinds of ladybugs eat the leaves of plants.

Larvae eat the same food as adult ladybugs. A grub will eat more than 200 aphids before it turns into a **pupa**.

Which animals attack ladybugs?

Ladybugs do not have many predators. Their bright color warns that they do not taste nice. Some kinds of spiders eat ladybugs.

Sometimes ants attack ladybugs and try to stop them from eating aphids. The ants want the aphids for their own food.

Where do ladybugs live?

Ladybugs live where they can find food to eat. They also need leaves where they can lay their eggs.

You will find ladybugs where there are lots of flowers or trees. They eat the aphids that live on the leaves or stems of the flowers.

How do ladybugs move?

Ladybugs use their wings to fly and look for food. When they land on a plant, they fold their wings under their wing-covers.

When a ladybug climbs up a stem it holds on with its six feet. It crawls very quickly to catch the aphids.

How long do ladybugs live?

Most ladybugs live through the spring, summer, and autumn. Many die in the cold winter because they cannot find enough food to eat.

Ladybugs do not like the cold weather. In the winter you may sometimes see them huddled together on the trunk of a tree or under a big stone.

What do ladybugs do?

People who have gardens like ladybugs because they eat pests. Pests harm the plants in gardens.

Sometimes farmers bring lots of ladybugs to their farms and **orchards**. The ladybugs eat aphids and other **insects** that kill the farmer's plants.

How are ladybugs special?

When a ladybug comes out of its **pupa**, its color is very pale and it has no spots. It takes about two days to become bright red with black spots.

Ladybugs do not have ears so they cannot hear. They can feel **vibrations** with their feet so they know if something is coming.

Thinking about Ladybugs

Do you remember what happens to the ladybug's eggs after she lays them?

How do ladybugs grow?

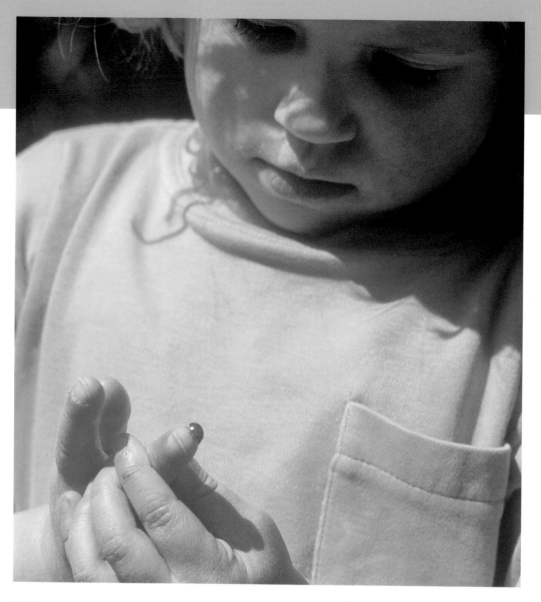

This child is going to look after some ladybugs. What do you think the ladybugs will need to eat?

Ladybug Map

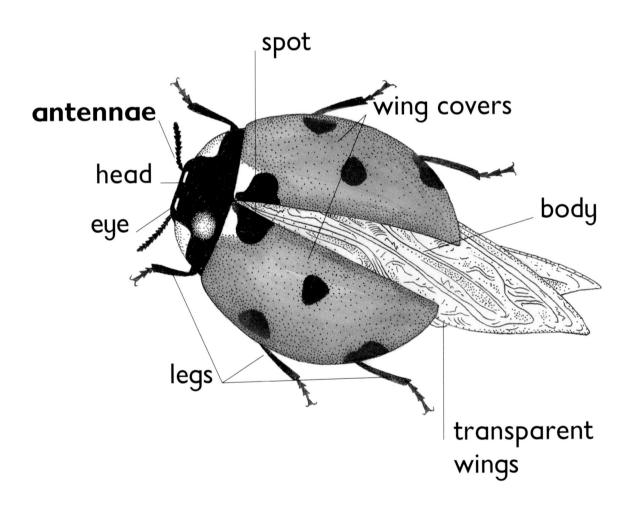

spot

antennae

wing covers

head

eye

body

legs

transparent
wings

Glossary

antenna (more than one are called **antennae**) two long thin tubes that stick out from the head of an insect. They may be used to smell, feel, or hear.

beetle an insect that has hard wing-covers to protect its wings

hatch to be born out of an egg

insect a small creature with six legs

larva (more than one are called **larvae**) the grub that hatches from the egg

molt when the larva grows too big for its skin it grows a new one and wriggles out of the old skin

orchard a place where farmers have planted lots of fruit trees

oval a shape that is almost round, like a squashed circle

pupa (more than one are called **pupae**) a step between larva and adult

vibration the moving that happens when something shakes

More Books to Read

Godkin, Celia. *What about Ladybugs?*
  San Francisco: Sierra, 1995.
Watts, Barrie. *Ladybug.* Columbus, OH: Silver Press,
  1991.

Index